JN440344

Following Birds

FOLLOWING BIRDS

A collection of new poems by Park Cheol
Translated by Jeon Seung-hee

Contents

FOLLOWING BIRDS

Following Winds

On my first visit to a trout farm—
As its owner sprinkled feed,
Fierce fighting,
Mouths gathered.

We scoop the trout
And have a lunch of them.

At an old temple site,
As the winds contribute to the offering,

How mountains faraway
Possess powers as red as flesh!

Hawkesbury River
—A Life

Sometimes I sit on a riverbank, where I can no longer visit,
And remain there, casting a fishing rod.
On that riverbank, where I stopped for no reason,
Following my wandering thoughts,
I sit alone and try to fish for an eel.
Because I arrived there late, after wandering around,
Darkness is approaching from across the river.

Still, as it's not entirely dark yet,
I sit staring at the end of the fishing rod,
Until everything in front of me disappears into darkness.
As if to reveal all the stillness and solitude,

Occasionally, a thick eel jumps up and writhes its body, in front of the setting sun,

At a remote outskirts of Sidney, where water soars,

Where nobody approaches and where even names retreat faraway.

To that river, which I can no longer visit,

I often find myself go unawares and sit on its bank.

I probably do not know, when I leave,

What I am waiting for or what will approach me

At that river with a common name,

Where everyone intentionally does not visit, although they know about it.

As our understanding of joys and sorrows are all

different,

No matter what we look at that is flowing,

There is only an empty heart that reaches the river and sits on its bank.

So there is no reason

I want to finally tell myself now.

At the Gimpo Public Library

Who was Giuseppe Chiara?*

A Jesuit priest from Sicily,

And the model for Father Sebastião Rodrigues, a protagonist in the novel *Silence*.**

Eventually capitulating to torture during his missionary work in Japan,

He became an apostate and lived 40 more years in exile in Edo

And died at 84.

* Giuseppe di Chiara (1602-85) was an Italian Jesuit missionary active in Japan when Christianity was strictly forbidden. He entered the country to locate a fellow priest, Cristóvão Ferreira, who had apostatized his Christian faith due to torture by Japanese authorities in 1633. Chiara was arrested in June 1643 and held for a time at a prison, the Kirishitan Yashiki, or the Christian Mansion at Edo. He was tortured and eventually became an apostate as well. He later married a Japanese woman, taking the name and samurai status of her late husband, Okamoto Sanemon, and lived in Japan until his death in 1685 in Edo [Translator's note].

** *Silence* is the title of the novel by Shusaku Endo [Translator's note].

But that he could not endure

Does not mean that he did not endure.

When I threw my head back, to take some cough medicine, while reading that part,

A title caught my eye from a bookshelf: *Rice Is Jesus*.

After finishing the act of taking a sip of water, I think:

A stopped cough does not necessarily mean no shaking.

I'll hold my breath until I have to be broken.

Then who is the god that I testify to?

Is my king still only you?

This was before I went out in search of a late lunch.

Following Birds

The reason for our gathering:
To see the group dance of a flock of Baikal teals
That flew down all the way from Siberia.

From Cheonsuman Bay in Seosan to the mouth of the Geumgang River,
From Dongnimji Pond in Gochang to the Gocheonam Seawall in Haenam,
We followed the birds southward.
Grand footsteps were left on the surface of the water
And we met only darkness wherever and whenever we arrived.
On that night we stayed in Julpo Port,
Having been chased in by darkness and cold;

They said there would be a reversal, their dance for us
Outside the veranda in the morning.
It's not an ordinary event to travel a long distance,
Like birds, following them,
But it's a path that once you take
You're bound to follow, even when you no longer want to.
We call it wintering
For a single point,
To survive, while burning alone,
They are simply staying at a place,
Like tears that eventually dry—

At any rate, the place we want to go

In order to follow the birds—

Did they say it's the place of mating?

Or a fate from which we cannot escape, no matter what?

Did they say a flock is one?

It cannot be only to convey the nature of the universe,

Where one depicts infinity,

That so many birds have vibrated

In the dark.

As I secretly know the reason why we should love,

I left my lodging before dawn,

Turning away from the "reversal," the dance.

Given the sound of moaning overnight,

Like that coming from those sleeping huddled in that room,
It seemed that a family of Eurasian coots was living there.
Could that have been the reversal?
When I saw in secret last night
The Chimhyangmu Dance the birds were doing,*
After leaving their simple life;
When I saw the greatest living being
In the universe
Like the candlelight during that winter,
My life was all but over.

* The Chimhyangmu Dance, meaning "dancing among agarwood incense," is the name of the dance people in Silla (57 B.C.E.-935) used to perform in front of Buddha. It became widely known due to the music composed and played by master musician of traditional Korean music Hwang Byung-ki (1936-2018). [Translator's Note]

I left the place without any doubt.

As I could measure the length of my life,

The lessons the group searched with me,

Fly the season that does not exist in this world.

Pull an oar that does not exist in this world.

Like coming out of my body,

Even if I don't ask what they were,

The sky was painted red again,

And when I returned, it was this morning.

Why Wonder Why It Snows in April?

Why does it snow in April?
After sending a fluttering photo like that,
I cannot make myself leave the edge of the water.

Why do I wonder why it snows in April?
So—do I mean it's not all right to snow in April;
It's not okay that it flutters in April?

Without withdrawing that one question,
I'm lingering, unable to dissolve.
Let's not think too much.
Let's not look at it for as long as it takes to think about it.
It has been only half a day since I emphatically promised myself.

And yet, like a home-comer who has missed the last train,
I throw up my arms,
Dumbfounded in front of this unexpected snow.

However, until so much snow ends up watching me,
Would there really have been such unexpected events in this world?
Couldn't it be that something cannot hold in anymore
And emerges as a certain, ultimate climax, even in this way?
April in Tasmania is fall,
And snow in April here, as spring is about to set.

However, both might be still looking at the same last winter.
The snow might be falling, erasing
The love I found only a few hours ago, after a long time.

Why does it snow in April?
White snow, gently announcing spring light,
Is dyeing the area around a dried mouth in yellow.
So, again feeling around letters that have left my fingertips,
Why do I wonder why it snows in April?
Do I mean it's not okay—
It's not all right that it flutters in April?
Why on earth do I wonder why it snows in April?

Li and Qi, the Two Origins

Faraway the curfew rang.

After the collar of winds has left, and while you're asleep,
And yet your heart still beats,
What do you do?
What do you do when your toenails are growing?
What do you do when the river of blood is flowing down?
When, at night, when even stars are asleep,
Your hair comes out through a rock,
When fine wrinkles appear one after another over your hardened face,
And struggles on the earth filling your soles are leaving the battleground,

When tears are trying to take a nap inside your eyelids,

When your liver sorts through noisy filth,

And when your calluses and bones straighten on their own,

When darkness goes on a journey,

And when your poor lung vessels are furiously blowing the bellows,

What do you do?

When only you are silently sitting next to you and guarding,

While the world, entirely unconcerned, is violently revolving outside the door,

When only you are standing next to you, facing yourself and crying,

When even you love yourself,
What do you do?
Do you not mind? Are you unconcerned?

At night, when the Milky Way inclines and the water wheel of the universe gently revolves,
And when even darkness loses its light and time is waiting for you,
What on earth would you do and where?
When, after wrapping yourself with ignorance, you put yourself into a mailbox,
What do you do?

When the whistle rings faraway?
When the siren washes over from faraway?

Snowflakes

I was on my way to see Mr. Hyun.*

It snowed, like a promise, like cow's eyes—
Cotton-like eyes waiting for a slaughter—

Now, silently, after a hard life under lashes,
Life as both a part of the whole and the whole of a part,

Like a lover who ran away after a great revolution,
A lover getting paid with sudden enlightenment and sudden practice, after working through gradual enlightenment and gradual practice,

* Hyun Ki Young is a South Korean novelist from Jeju province who wrote many stories dealing with the April 3 Jeju Massacre in 1948 and its aftermath. [Translator's note]

It snowed, and, passing by the entrance of Eulji-ro Street,
I stared for a while at the bullet marks on the old American Cultural Service building.

Only white snow was falling hurriedly, as if to keep a promise,
While a homeless man seemed deep in sleep under cardboard boxes meant for apples.

Perhaps because I grew up in a village near an airfield,
I am always in the midst of descending on the earth.

Meeting is like cotton bursting,

Parting is different from bullet marks.

The juvenile love affair in a translated poem without the original—

And I go to listen to belated regards, about which the sky clicks its tongue.

Although today I came down to the earth again out of fear,

I haven't yet landed like those big snowflakes.

Though I Love

On May 18th I saw spring leave.*

I could not—no, did not—detain it.

Only catching and walking under a drizzle,

I thought of a future of clear weather, but not when it would arrive.

Absurdly,

I would probably leave this world while singing blessings for a rain-cleared world.

I would probably leave saying goodbyes to everyone I met.

* May 18 indicates the Gwangju Uprising, a revolt in support of democratization in South Korea, which occurred in the southern city of Gwangju, from May 18 to May 27, 1980, and in which an estimated 1,000 people were killed protesting the martial law government. [Translator's note]

Such ominous thoughts come.
Without even opening my lips, although I love;
No,
Not even once having turned my eyes toward you; having lived while feeling as if unjustly treated or falsely accused,
I would likely become excited in my next life, too.

I think of love before love.
However, as if calling a person before the person,
I get angry, thinking of you while looking at the sky over Gimpo.
Since I began thinking, wiping my nose, a certain sky beyond the sky,
I have never reached the end of the road across

from me,

So, in fact, everyone else but you knows

That I have written poems all my life

In order to send Morse codes to you.

But it would be wonderful if someone now sent me even a bloody reply from May beyond May,

Letting me know who you are and where you are descending.

If I only knew

Whether there would be heavy rains and if Scops owls need to continue crying,

I wouldn't have to stand at the stern of a boat sailing with the sky in tow

And look at foam in the sea for a long time, like

this—

As the summer of gnats goes away and soon the season of winter hibernation comes,

Long live my dear revolutionary comrades, who were lost!

Gaehwa Checkpoint*

A few years before I read Kim Dong-in's "Flame Sonata,"**
I saw a lonely house at a remote corner of my village go up in flames.
Although villagers continued to relay buckets of water from the well,
In the end, the house was reduced to ashes.
When a checkpoint was being built on that site,

* Gaehwa Checkpoint is in front of my house, near the border between Seoul and Gyeonggi-do. During the military coup on December 12, 1979, the 1st Airborne troops could not have entered Seoul if the Capital Garrison Command had guarded this checkpoint, or if they had installed a barricade at the entrance to Haengju Daegyo Bridge while all the bridges over Han River were blocked. As the Capital Garrison Command overlooked the newly installed Haengju Dagyo Bridge, the 1st Airborne troops could enter Seoul, occupy the Ministry of Defense and Army Headquarters, and commit massacres in Gwangju the next year, followed by the establishment of the 5th Republic and the complete distortion of the flow of history.

** Kim Dong-in (1900-51) was an early pioneer of modern Korean fiction [Translator's note].

I climbed a hill behind Sanggeun's house and thought of "Flame Sonata" again.

It had been a long time since the owner of the house, my father's friend,

Had immigrated to Bolivia, after working hard for it; and occasionally passing by the site,

I saw only sweltering heat and heavy snow often pooling there.

Absurdly, in retrospect,

I feel heartache, thinking that the house was in a remote corner of the village.

As most people probably know, Kim Dong-in's short story concerns

A man who is wrapped up in extraordinary

excitement

While looking at wild flames in his years of deep-seated grudges.

Sometimes, whenever I get caught up in a vision
Where I am trapped at a checkpoint, in limbo,
And cannot escape this situation, for no reason,
And get beaten in a corner,
While my beloved looks on nearby,
I dart off to the hill in short steps,
Wishing that the world would be in flames.
As a farmer has to emigrate from the countryside to continue farming,
I sometimes would like to go far, far away, without a trace,
And live while listening to a sorrowful, fine sonata

like fireflies,

As Son Chang-seop did.*

* Son Chang-seop (1922-2010) was a renowned Korean novelist, active in the 1950s, best known for "Surplus Humans" (1958). In the early 1970s, he suddenly disappeared from the literary scene in Korea, to resurface in Japan in 2010, immediately before his death. It turned out that he had exiled to Japan with his Japanese wife in 1973 in the aftermath of the 1972 military coup.

The Gait of a Stork*

Not accidentally, most of my favorite poets
Led an unhappy life before dying.
After death, they tell me:
Don't live like me.

Living in seclusion in Patonga, past WoyWoy in Australia,
The novelist Don'O Kim was also an extreme aesthete.**
Although he had lived his entire life in seclusion and restraint,

* This title refers to a Korean proverb: "If a crow-tit tries to walk like a stork, he will break his legs," meaning: Tailor your ambitions to the measure of your abilities. [Translator's Note]

** Born in Pyongyang, Don'O Kim (Korean name: Kim Dong-ho; 1936-2013) is a Korean-Australian novelist. His novels include *The Chinaman*, *My Name is Tian*, and *The Grand Circle*.

What he said mostly to me in earnest was

Therefore, make lots of money.

My father was the same,

But all of them did not give up on themselves.

They gave me needless advice that I should live comfortably.

The only thing I learned from them was to take long strides, like that of a stork.

Like the back of a eucalyptus, like the skin of a snake,

Beautiful pretensions, flowing more thickly than watcr,

Unfold at the end of a sunset today as well.

They say, *Don't you live like me*. But,
Although they tell me not to live like them,
What else can I do?

About Another Light

Unexpectedly I've come to Seokmodo in Ganghwado Island.

To me, the mid-slope of Mt. Nakgasan seems like the bridge of a nose.

Out of breath, arriving finally at the Haesu Avalokitesvara site,

I plump down in front the statue.

The wind from the West Sea is delicate, and when breathlessly

I squat, I can see white mud flats through the stone railings, so close that it seems I could touch them;

Over a mud flat exposed at low tide,

Paths appear,

Cracks form,

And clear streams flow down.
They say that life is a mud flat, but from faraway
Mud flats are beautiful and brilliant—unlike the affairs of the world.

Toward a small island whose name I don't know,
Transmission towers are crossing,
Walking in giant strides,
Approaching in broad steps.
Things in front are flickering needlessly.
Yesterday, today, and after I leave,
The ironware will continue to cross, fluttering like that—
True towers.

At the site of prayer that I worked hard to reach,

Without really seeing the Buddha statue,

After only cowering in my breaths, I return, following the ebb tide.

Towers with hands firmly joined circle around the island.

A Clarinet and a Weeping Willow

—Summer 2014

My second child began to smile often
And repeatedly complained about his allowance. He was at that age.
I promised to give him a set amount of money every week.
As I didn't want to clash with him about it,
And as our mealtimes were different, I hid his allowance
Here and there in the house and then obliquely tipped him off about where to find it.
I wanted to give him memories for his future.
Money was tight, but it was convenient for both of us, and above all
It was fun, because he enjoyed it.

In fact, that allowance I gave him like a treasure hunt
Was all my household expenses.
Even while having myself blamed for being stingy,
It had a petty authority I wanted to show off before my child,
And my love for him like *pungran* orchids.
Even while I hid my poverty, which made me give up two-thirds of
The books I wanted to buy and two-thirds of the food I wanted to eat,
In the glow of the sun setting in the West Sea, in the month of winter solstice,
I felt it worthy, and never felt inconvenienced.

To begin with, my household expenses were Mother's tiny savings.

When I went to her home with groceries, or just absentmindedly,

My mother, in her 80s, would take my flip phone from me

And put a neatly folded $50 bill into its fold.

No matter how many times I waved, she was stubborn.

Sometimes when she found the bill she had put there before,

She would push another bill inside, saying, *My, look at you, look at you,*

How frugal you are!

So, sometimes, I had three or four of those bills

inside the fold of my phone,
And looking at Mother so happy about it, I would also chuckle foolishly.

In fact, Mother's tiny savings
Were the monthly rent of the man living in a small room she let;
The $200 that he took out of the basic living cost
The borough office made sure to send him every month;
A monthly rent that a man from somewhere in Jincheon
Regularly paid, a man who ended up there alone, after having been pushed from here and there.
A neat and desperate promise like his

housekeeping

And his early morning exercises, to do which he limped out, because of a cerebral hemorrhage.

In fact, the living cost he received and cherished

Was tax money the people had paid, sweet and vital money;

A cheerful snowball even to the care-worker who visited him every other week;

A solid and enormous mass like an iceberg, accumulated underwater,

The ditch water gathered slowly like tears,

Wherever it was melting,

Wherever it flowed down.

Snowflakes gather in a brooklet.

Sinheung Chicken, Pho Hoa, Saeson Stationary, Cheongryang Cleaners, and Seoseo Kalbi.

It was the spring water drawn up by a person chronically unemployed.

Whenever handfuls gathered at random shone as gold dust,

Gently stepping on the horseblocks in a thicket,

Where some are happy while others shed tears unawares of their feeling of unjust injury, I,

Like a weeping willow, cannot leave the side of a brook I came to love.

Sometimes I indulge in imagining

That I become a visiting conductor, wearing an

old tailcoat,

Happily swinging a baton toward the summit, while frequently glancing behind.

There my second child would blow a clarinet.

Insisting, *No, no, this is an oboe*,

He would sweat to keep pace with a player next to him.

Then, as if I would get back big-time at my child,

I would swing my arms even more forcefully, holding in my giggles.

Watching sparkling undulations managing to continue just a little at a time,

From white goosefoot and catkins to tearthumbs, asters, cattails, and silver grass,

He would be overwhelmed, *Wow, I didn't know*

Father was this great a personality!

He would be falling in love with the harmony of the orchestra to which I belong.

When we arrive at a time where we wash clumsy sounds in the stream and scoop them up one by one

And when our treasure hunt would no longer feel like fun—

In fact, that time had already come a while ago—

Then, please endlessly run around and around, brooklet.

And please find your dad in the end, my child.

In the distant future, the weeping willow will sway in a faraway place,

And that will be the everlasting history of my life.

Skill

1

A little distance from the river,
I saw the skill to make a fishing hook.
They were hands with deep creases
And stubby like pine mushrooms.
After bending a steel wire, they sharpened it in a grinder
And stood a barb straight
So that its end would be invisible.
The hook seemed like it would not hurt me
Even if I was caught in it.
While watching a tentacle,
Looking like a soft bone,
I thought of your fingertips.

2

There is no one who is not afraid of indelible sharpness.
I wonder which thick hands made your skill
Far away from me for a long time?
The mark left by those hands, the shock created by them—
It seemed that I would not die,
Even if I get caught in your skill like the light in your eyes.

3

I saw the skill to hand over a fishing hook
In the middle of a field path.
It was a hand that grasped the wind
On a high place under the sky.
It can catch everything.
We are all caught in it.
I seemed to have fallen for others
Like an icebreaker,
But in the end, I have devoted all my life to myself.
Because, while living, I could not part with myself,
How indeed I get caught by my own skill!
Until I realize that,
I wonder how many years and how far I have

travelled.

4

Thus, these days, as I have skimmed myself off, as I should do,

There is a flash of light whirling around in the air, cutting through my retina,

And it turns out you and I and he haven't yet left.

It turns out that you are still in the you of yours.

You are all gods.

The words I made sure to put on my fingertips in the wilderness yesterday,

We cannot run away!

Here I'd like to send you a short message.

5

As everyone
Becomes day and night,
And is sure to turn around,
We all
Go home,
Become earth.

Before we return,
Some are protagonists and others play supporting roles,
And still others are fishes, or sit on the riverside,

Nevertheless, it's all on a stage.

Even After Making Several Rounds in The Temple Yard, I Feel Bitter, As If I Have Completed My Life

In the Geomdansa Temple in Tanhyeon, along the riverbank, where the Imjin River and Han River meet,

There lives an elderly lay Buddhist, still with a solid build.

Whenever I go there, I find him sleeping, always sleeping.

Only after being approached cheerfully and called a few times,

He opens his left eye, stares at me, and then, dragging a long leash,

Gets up and greets me slowly, almost as if he's not actually greeting.

Only after I shout *Paw!* a few more times, he

pushes his paw to me,

But I say out of my lifelong, sorry feeling:

Please be born as a healthy human being in your next life!

As I say again uselessly such words, which I have said before,

He does not bother to finish listening and slowly goes back to where he was,

And, closing his left eye first, lies down at the bottom of the stone wall.

Near the rose mosses, with the prettiest sunrays in the temple yard,

Drink not the mineral water, but a whiff of winds, and, if you don't like even that,

Walk along the Gyoha bank, where this and that

ripple laps,

And leave after learning a lesson: Even if it's a loose one, a leash is a leash.

That's what he seems to say,

But still he never reveals his innermost thoughts, hidden in his old body.

Even after making several rounds in the temple yard, I still feel bitter, as if I have completed my life,

Thinking myself pathetic for repeatedly trying to hold the front paw of an old dog,

And wanting to come back repeatedly, even after I have seen him so many times,

I harass some leaves of a snowbell,

And walk down, after fully filling my chest with

clean air.

On such a day, when I feel a constant itchiness on my back, I cannot reach it with my hands.

Thus, I leave a poem here, titled:

An Old Dog at Geomdansa Temple.

Following Light

The color of the loneliness of an elderly man,
Who steals a few candies and begs to be arrested,
Must be that of a potato.
The color of the uniform of a young police officer, who tells him,
I cannot send you to prison for this,
And bows and asks about his relatives,
Must be indigo.
The color of the cover of history without beginning or end
Must be ochre,
While the color of the sigh of a ferryboat hovering near the bank,
With its arms crossed and its back against that of another ferryboat,

Must be that of off-white traditional *changhoji* paper.

However, nothing is done intentionally by anyone,
And no color is intentionally formed.
We can convey our hearts through flowers
Because colors run with them.
Within words as gentle as feelers,
Arise colors that cannot be pushed away, no matter how hard you try,
And storms that cannot be endured no matter what;
And the heart that was watching the disappearance of a family yesterday

Was the color of a blank look.
My son and his wife who have gone far, faraway,
In the spring when I was tired of myself,
And the fence of a quarry still in good condition,
That you can see, after turning the corner of the hill behind your house,
That looks like ants crawling up the stalks of roses,
Even if tomorrow is an off-day in an off-month of an off-year,
Must be the color of rusty water.

However, time does not return
To that faraway place from where I was supposed to have come.
Light a lamp, open the door, because I must

manage to live!

Today, after losing a color, which is also a light,

I am blinded

I am flooded

By too-bright a world.

Even so, tonight,

When I head to the prison with the speed of pitch-black color,

Is there really nobody who tries to hold onto me?

Ten Minutes

There's nothing as bland and abstract as time.
Like a person who keeps going, while drawing light,
Even after every being has left or become extinct,
There is no horse or ox as adamant as time.
In the winter of that year of a rampant pandemic, 2019,
A little past midnight,
I took a taxi to see her off.
Until we reached Noryangjin hill, after crossing Mapo Bridge,
We stared outside the window, forgetting words.
There is nothing as brilliant as the speechlessness that drives time,
Like the horse going forward while pulling

darkness.

As we reached our destination, the taxi stopped, like a half-moon,

And, suddenly, the driver hopped off, announcing, *I'll give you ten minutes*.

At this unexpected and sharp whistle breaking our silence, we could not respond,

So we were captivated for 10 more minutes, holding onto a fragment.

After a muddy time passed,

One got off, another got in, and another remained seated,

And we drove the Olympic Highway prostrate like time.

As if to announce my remaining life, as if to say

that life is all like this,
A long silence continued again along the road.
The unpaved road of time, full of
Many thoughts that I was used to during my lifetime,
Many words, bustles, the un-customariness of silence,
Black lights, was being pushed away.
After intentionally getting off at the entrance of the village,
I walked for a while again in silence,
And the taxi went away in silence,
And she must be asleep in silence.
Without anybody opening their mouth
About such overwhelming time, life was uselessly

Counting time. In it
I walked, continuing to tell myself that a short big-bang
Is a very long silence.

Shrimp

The child of the fritter house—As I loved the smell of oil always wafting from your body,

I, in the rented back-wing of a house in Yangnam-dong, looked at you with my hands on a worn-out threshold.

The overalls standing in the world as bright as the sun cut through the sliding door,

The child who looked back at me more often than the oil bubbles boiling up—

I scoop shrimp from your back even today, and my neck is bending.

I thank you for the smell of oil still wafting from you. Please be alive wherever you are.

How large is the sea that I can no longer visit, like the inside of the comforter of the sun where I spent midday?

Although it was very painful then, now my nose is happy just because of our bent backs.

From the road of the earth that I can continue to walk, to the faraway universe where I get lost,

I love that smell of oil that always returns to me with memories of you.

Seaside Cemetery

I once became lost among seaside sand dunes.

Three hours from Sidney,

Two younger friends had a hard time carrying snorkels and oxygen tanks under the scorching sun.

We continued to walk along the sand dunes and mangrove forests in more than 40 degrees Celsius.

Dumbfounded, we wondered what we'd been thinking on our way there,

Because our way back to the car seemed very far, much farther than our way here.

At the sound of waves, possibly approaching where we'd been,

I staggered while lifting my feet out of the sand.

Then my friends sat me down on a rock and went in different directions in search of the car.

It was a seaside cemetery I had observed only in films.

Overtaken by sudden exhaustion and terror,

In front of unfamiliar beds of death, which I experienced for the first time,

To erase the sense of isolation tightening around me, slowly,

I read epitaphs of the dead.

Knowing that I too might leave this world before long,

I could hear my lingering rough and blue feelings thronging above the sand dunes.

When, deserted between the seething, swimming in the sea and the cemetery, I

Was walking on the horizon of life and death,

I could see quite a number of old family graves,

Members of whom were born in quite different years,
But strangely died only a year or two apart.
Next to a child, a young mother was lain a year later,
Next to husband, a wife's name was added a half year later,
And elderly sisters who died less than two years apart.

I learned that missing was scarier than hunger;
Indeed, how they must have been unable to give up their love in the end!

When I was holding onto deaths that hastily followed one another, with my entire body,
And wondering who would follow me soon after my departure,
I eventually felt stupefied,
When, far off, letting me know that it was still hot,
A car horn sounded.

Loving White Snow

While waiting for the bus,
I secretly leave a footprint
On a pure white snow mound waiting for the spring,
Leaning on the base of a gingko tree—
That's how clumsily I think of you.

It has been about a month since Daehan,*
And four days since the heavy snowfall, and it is warmer today, so
How can this snow mound be so white and beautiful?
After the door of the sky opened shyly,
As the notes I sent to you endlessly returned,

* Daehan, meaning "Great Cold," is the 24th of the 24 seasonal divisions, usually occurring around January 20. [Translator's note]

Like stones thrown by the innocent,
Although you must have let yourself stay in my arms that night,
While gasping because of the hands that would not stop,
Let's go to the earth, let's go to the earth,
Indeed, you could not turn around for all the world!
Suddenly, my eyes become swollen.
And even my ears get warmed blackish red.
When the bus arrives, the footsteps are erased,
Spring flowers bloom, and gingko leaves cry in yellow,
Please don't forget me, as I won't forget you.
While greeting today,

While wandering helplessly, not knowing how to live,
Oh, how many icy blasts and heat waves have passed,
And chopped at the backs of my feet!

Two Widows

Perhaps we should rather have performed the funeral rite in front of the cowshed.
But Mother deliberately dragged a cow with psoriasis and stood it in front of the bier.
She was saying, *You cannot do this to your wife*.

On the day when Father passed away in Yeonbaek
I hear that both the cow and Mother cried
As the cow's nose-ring looked particularly big.

This is what I heard
From an elderly lady in a chophouse in Gochon.

We Should First Get Rid of That Darned Road

—A Night When I Think of Kim Su-yeong After a Long While

There are people who make a detour
Of a short road,

While there are those who dash off in a stride
Even on a long road.
However,
They all arrive at the same place.

People are busy going,

Become blind running away,
And go all over the places to die, but

The world is the size of a sole, no matter how far you go.

As long as there is a road,
That is a problem.
We should first get rid of that darned bright road.

We should erase first the lines,
Overturn the *go* boards,
And throw stones.

Don't love.
Don't pray.
How to die forever while you live.
How to live forever after you die.
Above all, we should bury those darned stupid maxims.

POET'S NOTE

— They say poems should not be written honestly. But I try to write honestly. In today's environment, my poems are classical. Awhile ago, a long, long time ago, they were considered new. In order to not throw away the obsolete, old way, I spend new time in a new way everyday. Everything is both new and becomes old. What is important should be how to let both facts remain fresh in one's heart. Not in my heart, but in that blue sky.

— I cultivate a field and sow seeds. As I have been dragging only letters, how I have been stupider than oxen! It's now time to listen to the thoughts of letters, too.

— Rather than the "arbitrary optimism" that I heard Edward Said believed in his late years, I trust more the instinctive, innate optimism of the homeless, who try to cover themselves even with sheets of newspaper. I suppose it has something to do with value; but then, only God knows what and which human life is more precious and profound than others. So there's no need for us to try to figure it out.

— My thoughts are not free. That's because they are imprisoned in the material holocaust. Things will probably be different after survival. When the thought becomes narrow, the space between lines becomes narrow, too.

— Don't be imprisoned in too big a word. Worries about insurance premiums, monthly rents, and maintenance fees. What is big is within what is small.

— Chefs of letters, please listen to the words of

high-end gourmets for once! But, then, there aren't many gourmets as fastidious as oneself.

— Although rivers seem to fill the sea, it is the endless sea that provides their fund.

— Zen requires concentration and cutting off all idle (and harmful) thoughts, but poetry should be able to cut off all idle thoughts. It should help one reach the state of straight thought without evil. Writing poems is "sudden enlightenment and gradual cultivation" while the poetry should be "sudden enlightenment and sudden cultivation."

Poetry is born selfishly and lives altruistically.

— Poetry is in the end a matter of power.

— Messages, thoughts, and skills. In the end,

what matters is technique. Even a rebar worker needs technique.

— I sometimes find myself saying it is difficult to write poems. It's when they are running away, already far into the future. Poems want to be thrown farther and farther away from reality. It is arrogant and difficult work to drag them and place them in front of a dinner table or just stop them. After letting poems do whatever they want, I should just say, hmm, this was hard. That should be enough. Even if a poem is good, I don't need to say that it's good, because it's already good.

— The language barrier of course concerns communication. I think what's blocked is more reason than feeling. What can be translated in poetry would be not reason but fragments of feeling or sentiments. Reading a book about D.H. Lawrence falteringly, I thought that this thick book might someday be translated into another language, but that it could not be understood fully. However, how great it is to exchange even some feelings! That's why the sound of crying after someone has passed away is so sorrowful.

— In the late 1980s, I began reading *Duman River*, a novel by Ri Ki-yong Minchon, often called the "Korean Gorky," but I could not finish it. It was too long. Lenin's comrade Gorky served Stalin. Boris Akunin, a super-rich Russian novelist, once said that Gorky could have been the best Russian novelist if he had died 10 years earlier than he did. Akunin seems, however, to absolutely trust the money that he serves. I prefer Stalin's statement that an author is a construction worker building human hearts. By saying that, I of course don't mean that I can become a member of the heart construction workers' union.

— There are times when loneliness shines brightly. The times when you worry about yesterday's forests.

— To be beneficial means to not rule.

— Globalization is not harmony, but reproduction and simplification. It is good to endlessly recite poems by Yun Dong-ju,[13] but it is more important to write more, different poems by Yun Dong-ju. True abundance is not

13 Yun Dong-ju (1917-45) was a Korean poet born in Longjing, China during the Japanese colonial era. He was known for his lyrical and resistance poems against Japanese colonialism. He died in February 1945 in Fukuoka Prison in Japan. [Translator's Note]

impossible.

— 70% of *minjung* poems are abstract.[14]

— People who don't have challenges in their everyday lives seek challenges in vacations.

— People with a good education should make more efforts to be humble—as if they have criminal records. They exist in a state highly unfavorable to knowing how to be humble.

— Concepts of labor and laborer need to be better defined, like the concept of religion. The dehumanization of simple labor, as mentioned

14 *Minjung* is a Korean word that combines the two Chinese characters *min* and *jung*, meaning "the people" and "the public." Thus, *minjung* can be translated as "the masses" or "the people." Culturally, the word denotes people who are oppressed politically, exploited economically, marginalized socially, and despised culturally. Thus *minjung* poems are poems depicting their conditions in order to represent and advocate for them. [Translator's Note]

by Marx and Charlie Chaplin. Saying that there is no labor in me is as humiliating as saying there is no brain in a laborer. Creative writing that reproduces itself excessively exists, above all, outside the field of labor.

— Metaphorization that does not follow hope but progresses while treading despair. That's not because humans are weak, beautiful, cowardly, or colorful, but because that's how humans pray. Humans cannot help fluttering according to the way they are looked at, how they are hung on the clothesline.

— A masterpiece envies the fate of its author. Yet even ghosts forget that they are ghosts.

— I hear that I am destined to become a public official in the other world, so let me endure life with hope, even if a meager hope. My belief that a poem can break a rock was a vain one. Not the poem, but the belief. Rather than struggling to find belief, all I should do is to just reach into a corner of myself and take it out.

— Readers are not users. A poet tries often to have readers *do* something. When we barely manage to assemble dismantled parts, some shape *does* emerge, but that doesn't mean it works.

— Neither witticism, nor ideas, nor volubility, nor aphorisms are poems. This is true of episodes as well. All of them need to be sitting side by side with clammy scenes of individual lives, their reality.

— Attention and indifference...forcibly and unawares.

If writing is done forcibly, it does not deserve big praise, even if its result is good; if a piece of writing is done poorly unawares, it also does not deserve big blame.

— Robert Walser passed away on a snowy road on a Christmas day in 1956, after wandering around mental hospitals and nursing homes for 28 years. He probably could not imagine that I would read his writings in a remote place entirely unrelated to him after a long time. It was not necessary to imagine it. Every time I think about this, I feel as if I'm looking at the stars in the night sky. Whenever I look at a star that may no longer exist, the star will mostly tell me this: Why should I look at the star?

— Someday, the sea will dry up as well. Today, the sea has barely managed to be beautiful. I could see the sea because you existed.

— Even just because the phenomenon and pre-phenomenon, painting and space, crying and echoes, meditations and messages hold their breaths in my poems, they can be called "impressionist" poems.

— No matter how anxious, you cannot grab water in order to drink it. You have to hug tightly, but not necessarily with both hands. Most people envy thoughtless people.

— *Li* or *qi*? It's not easy to figure out which precedes which, but I'm more curious if scholars really fought so fiercely about this question.[15] Last spring, I visited houses of mourning many times, as befits my age. Where are traces of the person I spent a long time together with and whose hand I held only a few days ago? I thought, Oh, that must be why they fought! That could happen. Hills I used to look at have disappeared and high rises replaced them. Those ancestors could not have seen excavators, but they must have fought so desperately because they knew the way of the world just by looking at the way flowers bloomed and fell.

— As what I dream about does not exist in this world, it is natural that the end of truth-seeking is destruction. Deprived of all

15 During the mid- to late Joseon period, neo-Confucian scholars engaged in heated philosophical debates on the precedence between *li* (theory) and *qi* (energy), which even caused the persecution of groups of Confucian scholars in the opposing sides. [Translator's Note]

obsessions and desires, after breaking them into pieces, I only watch the end of the public square, an empty alley.

— No false charge is as serious as locking oneself into the prison-house of one's mind. How we judge and imprison ourselves! Not doing and being unable to do—only humans can't distinguish them.

— Sweating is a good thing. However, it's a shame that only humans sweat.

— An ideology is not created but evolves. With pains, you go on a different way; but without pains, you walk only along time. Unchanging gestures are worse than pain.

— You cannot talk about dreams without

dreaming. But a dream is a dream only after you're outside of it. This is true of a poem as well.

— My sincerity would be the size of myself in the universe, but its voice would go forward as far as it would fly into the universe, from where it cannot return.

— When dry leaves touch the earth, when they touch the earth no longer as fallen leaves but as signs, all sentences must be completed and read. Life is also a mere sign. Thinking of Kim Jong-chul, an ecologist is a rationalist.[16]

— We all know where we're imprisoned and why.

16 Kim Jong-chul (1947-2020) was a literary critic and pioneering ecological thinker in Korea who founded the bimonthly *Green Review* in 1991. [Translator's Note]

Now, the exit is an only exit. Therefore, we should be quiet, leaving confusion behind, for the sake of vain time, which will not be in vain. We should be humble. Being oxidizes understanding.

— Literature is only a scout, and there is no scout who steps forward toward in world only as an experiment. How scary it is to predict thoughts! What I want to say is to kill words that cannot be said with words. This may sound absurd, but I cannot find other ways to say it. Such silence. The irony of having lived to death is truly poetic.

COMMENTARY

POET

Pursuing Supreme Enlightenment at the Edge of the Abyss

Hong Gi-don (Literary Critic)

The way Park Cheol summons faraway things to scenes in the here and now could be called the pursuit of supreme enlightenment at the edge of life's abyss in the Buddhist sense. The first poem in this book, "Following Winds," illustrates this point well: "On my first visit to a trout farm—/As its owner sprinkled feed,/Fierce fighting,/Mouths gathered.//We scoop the trout/And have a lunch of them.//At an old temple site,/As the winds contribute to the offering,//How mountains faraway/Possess powers as red as flesh!" (entire text). The trout farm calmly introduced in the first stanza denotes a scene where our lives are unfolding. Would it be only the trout that fight for feed? The poet's concern, however, is not the scene of fighting, but what is beyond all fights.

Regardless of victory or defeat, all things alive are destined to descend to death—just as the trout that were fiercely fighting end up as a dish on a lunch table. At this point, the sense of distance emerges in the word "faraway," when we're reminded of such a course of life. The mountains are a symbol of nature embracing and nurturing all lives. The last stanza describes the mountains covered with fall foliage as being red and in an exclamatory tone. As fighting is the basic way of life, that vitality throbs with life in "red as flesh." And it is because nature contains such vitality that its movement is also recognized as being red. Of course, the vitality will eventually end up being exhausted, corresponding to the expected course of fall heading into winter. That must be why the enlightenment of the moment, when a scene at a trout farm is caught in the poetic speaker's pursuit of supreme enlightenment, led to an exclamation about how red it is.

Other poems emphasizing the pursuit of supreme enlightenment at the edge of life's abyss include "Skill," "Following Birds," "Following Light." As an owner is sprinkling feed in a trout farm, in "Skill," there is also a being who, "[a]fter bending a steel wire,…sharpened it in a grinder/And stood a barb straight/So that its end would be invisible" in a scene of life and death. The "hand that grasped the wind/On a high place under the sky" would be the Creator—who controls both the absoluteness of the "sky," which also means "heaven" in Korean, and the nothingness of the wind. That is why no one is free from the fishing hook he makes: "*It can catch everything./We are all caught in it.*" "Skill" is a poem that describes life's abyss through personification.

In "Following Birds," the abyss unfolds as the origin of a long journey. Siberia, evoked in "a flock of Baikal teals/That flew down all the way from Siberia," reminds us of life's abyss. Its barren environment evokes life's origin, but its Lake Baikal was the origin where ancestors of the Korean, Mongolian, and Japanese peoples lived during the Paleolithic era. Thus, the migration of the flock of Baikal teals represents the destiny of all beings, expressed in: "It's not an ordinary event to travel a long distance,/Like birds, following them,/But it's a path that once you take/You're bound to follow, even when you no longer want to." The end of this journey that began at abyss would also be the edge: "We call it wintering/For a single point,/To survive, while burning alone,/They are simply staying at a place,/Like tears that eventually dry."

Then, what meaning does life sliding from edge to edge have? The poet finds an answer in the group dance of Baikal teals unfolding on the opposite side of "a family of Eurasian coots" living a simple life near a lake: "When I saw in secret last night/The Chimhyangmu Dance the birds were doing, /After leaving their simple life;/When I saw the greatest living being/In the universe/Like the candlelight during that winter,/My life was all but over." The Chimhyangmu Dance, expressed in the group dance of Baikal teals, symbolizes the eternity of life. In other words, while witnessing the group dance of Baikal teals, the poetic speaker must have felt the meaning of life overcoming the limits of individual lives. We can judge from his will to "*[f]ly the season that does not exist in this world*" that his orientation is the same as that of the Baikal teals' journey—a will to go beyond the life of Eurasian coots that are satisfied with a simple life near a lake, a life that's similar to that of trout in a farm.

"Following Light" is a poem about the color of

the world we live in, which is seen as varied: "The color of the loneliness of an elderly man,/Who steals a few candies and begs to be arrested,/Must be that of a potato./The color of the uniform of a young police officer, who tells him,/*I cannot send you to prison for this*,/And bows and asks about his relatives,/Must be indigo./The color of the cover of history without beginning or end/Must be ochre,/ While the color of the sigh of a ferryboat hovering near the bank,/With its arms crossed and its back against that of another ferryboat,/Must be that of off-white traditional *changhoji* paper." Also, "the fence of a quarry" is "the color of rusty water." But all these colors in our lives originate from black. That is, the color of the abyss is black—this explains why the poetic speaker understands the speed of life's irreversible direction as "pitch-black" in his describing life as "head[ing] to the prison with the speed of pitch-black color" from "that faraway place from where I was supposed to have come." To Park Cheol, life unfolds right at the edge of the abyss.

The statement in "Following Light" that various colors, that is, various concrete shapes of life, originated fundamentally from black is noteworthy. It shows Park Cheol's attitude toward the world as he understands it, above all, focusing on senses and feelings. Park's critical attitude toward this world, which is primarily based on reason in its workings, can be found in the poem "We Should First Get Rid of That Darned Road."

Park wants to go beyond the order of the modern world constructed according to a scientific worldview. If "Mr. Mateo Tunari of the Machigenga Tribe" is a person "who make a detour/Of a short road," modern men with much knowledge would be "those who dash off in a stride/Even on a long road." Despite differences in their lifestyles, both "arrive at the same place," that is, the abyss. Nevertheless, "People are busy going,/ Become blind running away,/And go all over the places to die." Park Cheol wrote "We Should First Get Rid of That Darned Road" where he wants to block the road that appears to unfold brightly in front of us. When he says, "We should first get rid of that darned bright road," and then declares, "Above all, we should bury those darned stupid maxims," both of them represent fundamental principles of our modern life.

Perhaps only after we let our reason sleep a little might we be able to realize many things about life. For example, in "*Li* and *Qi*, the Two Origins", they exist "while you're asleep,/And yet your heart still beats," "when your toenails are growing," "when the river of blood is flowing down, and "When your liver sorts through noisy filth,/And when your calluses and bones straighten on their own." This is also the time "when the Milky Way inclines and the water wheel of the universe gently revolves,/ And when even darkness loses its light and time is waiting for you." In other words, it's a message that, only when we reach the time when we escape from inveterate rationalism we can fully recognize ourselves as living and achieve unity with all things in the universe. In these moments, demanding a revolution in our way of life, as if to awaken us, the "curfew," "whistle," and "siren" ring and the poet asks us: "What do you do?//When the whistle rings faraway?/When the siren washes over from faraway?" The poem "*Li* and *Qi*, the Two Origins" seems to argue that *qi*'s value should be restored or that *qi* precedes *li*.

As Park Cheol understands the world from the perspective of life, or living beings, it is natural that he pursues the direction in which we become unified with nature. It is to emphasize the uniqueness of humanity that we focus on reason, while it is at a place where we embrace the possibility of coexistence with all other beings that we focus on life.

K-POET
Following Birds

Written by Park Cheol
Translated by Jeon Seung-hee
Published by ASIA Publishers
Address 445, Hoedong-gil, Paju-si, Gyeonggi-do, Korea
Tel (8231).955.7958
Fax (8231).955.7956
Email bookasia@hanmail.net
Homepage Address www.bookasia.org

ISBN 979-11-5662-317-5 (set) | 979-11-5662-592-6 (04810)
First published in Korea by ASIA Publishers 2022

This book is published with the support of the Literature Translation Institute of Korea (LTI Korea).

K-Fiction series

최근에 발표된 단편소설 중 가장 우수하고 흥미로운 작품을 엄선하여 출간하는 〈K-픽션〉은 한국문학의 생생한 현장을 국내외 독자들과 실시간으로 공유하고자 기획되었습니다. 원작의 재미와 품격을 최대한 살린 〈K-픽션〉 시리즈는 매 계절마다 새로운 작품을 선보입니다.

001 버핏과의 저녁 식사-**박민규** Dinner with Buffett-**Park Min-gyu**
002 아르판-**박형서** Arpan-**Park hyoung su**
003 애드벌룬-**손보미** Hot Air Balloon-**Son Bo-mi**
004 나의 클린트 이스트우드-**오한기** My Clint Eastwood-**Oh Han-ki**
005 이베리아의 전갈-**최민우** Dishonored-**Choi Min-woo**
006 양의 미래-**황정은** Kong' s Garden-**Hwang Jung-eun**
007 대니-**윤이형** Danny-**Yun I-hyeong**
008 퇴근-**천명관** Homecoming-**Cheon Myeong-kwan**
009 옥화-**금희** Ok-hwa-**Geum Hee**
010 시차-**백수린** Time Difference-**Baik Sou linne**
011 올드 맨 리버-**이장욱** Old Man River-**Lee Jang-wook**
012 권순찬과 착한 사람들-**이기호** Kwon Sun-chan and Nice People-**Lee Ki-ho**
013 알바생 자르기-**장강명** Fired-**Chang Kangmyoung**
014 어디로 가고 싶으신가요-**김애란** Where Would You Like To Go?-**Kim Ae-ran**
015 세상에서 가장 비싼 소설-**김민정** The World' s Most Expensive Novel-**Kim Min-jung**
016 체스의 모든 것-**김금희** Everything About Chess-**Kim Keum-hee**
017 할로윈-**정한아** Halloween-**Chung Han-ah**
018 그 여름-**최은영** The Summer-**Choi Eunyoung**
019 어느 피씨주의자의 종생기-**구병모** The Story of P.C.-**Gu Byeong-mo**
020 모르는 영역-**권여선** An Unknown Realm-**Kwon Yeo-sun**
021 4월의 눈-**손원평** April Snow-**Sohn Won-pyung**
022 서우-**강화길** Seo-u-**Kang Hwa-gil**
023 가출-**조남주** Run Away-**Cho Nam-joo**
024 연애의 감정학-**백영옥** How to Break Up Like a Winner-**Baek Young-ok**
025 창모-**우다영** Chang-mo-**Woo Da-young**
026 검은 방-**정지아** The Black Room-**Jeong Ji-a**
027 도쿄의 마야-**장류진** Maya in Tokyo-**Jang Ryu-jin**
028 홀리데이 홈-**편혜영** Holiday Home-**Pyun Hye-young**
029 해피 투게더-**서장원** Happy Together-**Seo Jang-won**
030 골드러시-**서수진** Gold Rush-**Seo Su-jin**
031 당신이 보고 싶어하는 세상-**장강명** The World You Want to See-**Chang Kang-Myoung**